AU ME

A Story of Strength, Perseverance and Faith

AUTHENTIC ME

A Story of Strength, Perseverance and Faith

Tiffany Hill

EXPECTED END ENTERTAINMENT

Atlanta, GA

Copyright © 2015 Tiffany Hill
All rights reserved. No part of this book may be reproduced or transmitted in any form or by any means, electronic or mechanical, including photocopy, recording, or by any information storage and retrieval system with the exception of a reviewer who may quote brief passages in a review to be printed in a blog, newspaper or magazine without written permission from the author. Address inquiries to: Expected End Entertainment, P.O. Box 1751, Mableton, GA 30126.
Published by Expected End Entertainment/EX3 Books
info@EX3Books.com * www.EX3Books.com
Names, characters, businesses, places, events and incidents are used in a fictitious manner.
ISBN-10: 0996893202
ISBN-13: 978-0-9968932-0-6
Printed in the United States of America

DEDICATION

This book is dedicated to my 3T's who have shown me the true meaning of genuine, unrelenting love.

ENDORSEMENTS

"I've heard that thousands of women suffer in silence daily from physical and/or emotional abuse. I pray that Tiffany Hill's book, *Authentic Me*, will give other women the courage they need to step out of the darkness and start living the life of freedom that they all deserve."

Author Lorna L.A. Lewis
Baton Rogue, LA

"*Authentic Me* is a riveting story of personal growth in the face of challenges. The main character exemplifies strength and a willingness to push through her pain and heal. This book is a must read!"

Marquette Young, J.D.
Houston, TX

"*Authentic Me* inspires through raw honesty. It challenges the reader to know who you are and love who you are. It will truly empower anyone on a path to finding their authentic selves."

Stephanie Findley
Bernice, LA

"*Authentic Me* represents the many voices of women who have not yet found courage to move beyond the present and tell their story. It's a book that compels conversation."

Author Necole Turner
Atlanta, GA

TABLE OF CONTENTS

INTRODUCTION ix

CHAPTER 1
LOVE MARRIAGE, AND A BABY CARRIAGE 1

CHAPTER 2
WELCOME TO CAMPUS LIFE 15

CHAPTER 3
PRIVATE LIFE vs. PUBLIC LIES 23

CHAPTER 4
SHOWTIME! 41

CHAPTER 5
HOMOPHOBIA 53

CHAPTER 6
BREAKING POINT 65

CHAPTER 7
FULL CIRCLE 77

CHAPTER 8
MOVING FORWARD, AUTHENTICALLY 85

EPILOGUE
SO YOU'VE BEEN ABUSED 91

ABOUT THE AUTHOR 97

TIFFANY HILL

INTRODUCTION

Life happens, and rarely goes according to plan. There are moments when you face problems that seem insurmountable. Your faith is tested. You find yourself broken and wonder if you can continue on. You begrudgingly begin each day and cover your pain with a mask. Underneath the mask lies the authentic truth of who you are.

Authentic Me details a story filled with turmoil as emotional experiences of domestic abuse and infidelity are revealed. A marriage to Kyle causes the main character to be thrust into a series of public roles. Their lives become a whirlwind of public events and publicity stunts, and she is the star of the performance. Failure to perform at her full potential results in abuse. Those who should protect her become enablers of further abusive situations. The message is clear: she should remain silent or suffer the consequences.

Her failure to acquiesce would force her to pay the ultimate price as she finds herself in a custody battle for her children. At her breaking point, she must decide whether to succumb to defeat or live victoriously. The choice is hers.

To save herself, she taps into her faith and reconnects to the core of who she is. She quickly realizes that her healing must be purposeful and will only begin once she uncovers the mask, peels away the hurt layer by layer and lives her truth.

Chapter 1

LOVE, MARRIAGE AND A BABY CARRIAGE

"Each new morning you get to write a new page in the present chapter of your life book. Make sure today that you are writing powerfully, purposefully and passionately. This is your life. You are the author of your story."

~ Sophia A. Nelson

I will never forget the moment I discovered I was pregnant with my first child. I was so excited! The excitement was displayed through tears of joy which immediately turned to worry. Would I have a normal pregnancy? Would the baby be healthy? How would the delivery go? How would I handle being a new mom? My worry turned into fear. Yikes! Will I really have to push a baby out? How much will the baby weigh?

As the questions plagued my mind, my level of anxiety heightened. Labor and delivery shows made me nervous. I had nightmares about horrific delivery procedures and baby abnormalities. I was totally elated about the pregnancy all while being completely terrified of childbirth. Well, it was too late for that fear now. The baby was inside of me growing and doing well. At some point, a precious newborn would make their debut into the world, whether this mommy-to-be was nervous or not.

I soon learned I was giving birth to a baby boy. The joy of it was indescribable. I wanted everything to be perfect for him. The nursery had to be color coordinated and fully equipped with the baby essentials: the crib, car seat, stroller and other newborn baby items, all of which would be selected only after reading consumer safety reports and endless customer reviews. I was anxiously preparing for motherhood, my first child. It had to be perfect and according to plan.

Later, I began having complications with the pregnancy. My heart literally stopped beating for a moment. Preeclampsia was the diagnosis. No surprise. It was indeed a stressful time. I was newly married. I had recently relocated, started a new job and was getting settled into a new home. I was also studying for the Michigan bar examination.

As a result of the preeclampsia diagnosis, the doctor ordered bed rest. Bed rest?! I thought, "What exactly does that entail?" Maybe I hadn't fully explained to the doctor the extent of what I had going on and how busy I was. I couldn't possibly put aside all of my responsibilities and be confined to a bed! In hindsight, I now know it was something I should have welcomed as a break from the fast pace of my chaotic world.

*****

My husband Kyle, whose career was in higher education, had recently secured a position as the student affairs administrator at a university in Michigan. We lived in a small college town and hadn't been there long enough for me to establish a strong support network. I was nervous about being there without family support, especially after experiencing sickness during the pregnancy.

When I gave birth, my mother came in town to stay with us for a few weeks. My son was born premature and remained in the neonatal intensive care unit of the hospital for two weeks after I was discharged. The drive from our home to the hospital was one and a half hours. Rather than make the long drive daily, my mom and I opted to lodge in a nearby hotel to be close to the hospital.

My baby was perfect in my eyes. I spent so much time at the hospital to the point that my mother began to encourage me to go to the hotel and rest for a few hours in between visits. I couldn't understand why Kyle wasn't as equally excited about the baby as I was and wondered if it would be unfair to him to raise it as an issue. He was certainly busy at work. Perhaps I was overreacting. He was a male, which in my opinion somehow made him less compassionate. I was worried and concerned for the baby and decided not to let my apprehension spill over into our marriage.

When Kyle stopped by for a visit, he informed me that he would be traveling to attend a student affairs conference the next day. So much for avoiding an argument! The baby was only a few days old and was being fed through a feeding tube. It was insensitive to consider leaving with the baby in that condition.

"You've got to be kidding me! You're going to leave while our newborn baby is in the hospital to go to a conference that is conveniently in the city where your mistress lives? Is Dana that important?"

Dana and Kyle had a long history. They dated prior to our relationship and were once engaged to be married. They went a period of time with no communication, but Dana resurfaced when she discovered that Kyle and I were married. She professed her love for Kyle and the regret of not following through with their plans for marriage. Initially, Kyle was very open with me about Dana and set boundaries between them. Later, the phone calls increased in frequency and an intimate relationship developed.

Although I was agitated, I remained cognizant of the fact that the baby could sense tension. He needed us to be attentive to him, not arguing in his presence. I committed to blocking out the marital frustrations and becoming solely focused on the baby's needs.

I was basking in the joy of being a new mom. I couldn't be more amazed that I'd given birth to someone who depended on me for everything. The feeling was surreal. My prayers had been answered. The baby made much progress during his stay in the hospital. He was a healthy, happy bundle of joy and that was all that mattered to me.

The day he was discharged and able to come home was one of the happiest days of my life.

*****

Honestly, this wasn't my first pregnancy. A few months before I started law school, I became pregnant by my high school boyfriend. The timing of that news could not have been worse. I was at a point where I was ready to fulfill my dream of being an attorney, but how could I accomplish that task with a newborn baby? Did I even want to try? I decided that I did not. I had an abortion.

I never spoke with anyone about the abortion which consequently allowed me not to have to deal with the emotions that came along with my choice. It didn't occur to me that a single selfish act would shape my future decisions. When I was faced with difficult problems later in life, I resorted to that comfortable mechanism of handling issues: avoidance.

Years later those emotions surfaced, causing me to remain in an abusive marriage and aiding in the process of my self-worth being devalued. I believed that domestic abuse was the punishment for my previous mistake. I'd killed an innocent being to pursue my professional dreams and aspirations. When I married, I had the lifestyle I longed for yet had the audacity to be unhappy when it came with additional baggage. Would years of physical, emotional and financial abuse be the price I paid for the fairytale lifestyle I desired or was it too much to endure? I often questioned myself, yet there was little time for a pity party. I'd dealt myself these cards and now it was time to play my hand. I learned to play my hand very well. I would even argue that I became too good at playing the game, at the expense of denying myself the authenticity and happiness I deserved.

*****

"You're a stupid bitch!" he yelled, before he hit me so hard in my face that he knocked me down onto the living room floor. It took a second for the reality of the moment to set in. When it finally did, my mind immediately went into overdrive. I was angry! This motherfucker actually hit me! Truthfully, the fact that he hit me wasn't what I was most upset about. I was furious he called me a bitch!

"I know you didn't just call me a bitch! Have you lost your mind?" I stormed over to the closest telephone to dial 911. He wouldn't call me a bitch and hit me in the process! He was going to pay for this!

Kyle pleaded with me not to call the police. My head was pounding so his requests sounded like distorted rambling. "I'll leave," he said. "We don't need people in our business. Think about our jobs. How embarrassing would it be for everyone to know that we had a fight?"

In my mind I thought, we didn't have a fight. You hit me. You called me a bitch. You lost your temper. It's not my fault!

"911 what's your emergency?" the dispatcher asked.

"My husband and I were arguing and he hit me in the face," I replied. I burst into tears. The dispatcher requested that I remain on the telephone as she sent a police officer to our home.

As I held the telephone receiver, I became sick to my stomach. I was dizzy and felt an overwhelming urge to vomit. I was very afraid. Had I overreacted? I'd called the police on my son's father, my husband. I certainly didn't want him to go to jail. What kind of person would that make me? I hung up the telephone.

My mother-in-law was in town visiting which added tension in and of itself. After hearing all of the commotion, she rushed into the room where we were. Kyle gave his mother a brief synopsis of what had taken place. She immediately began orchestrating our talking points for the police.

"Neither of you should put your jobs in jeopardy over a silly argument," she said. "When the officers arrive, you should tell them it was just a misunderstanding. Do not agree to press charges. The last thing you need is police involved in your private affairs."

I couldn't comprehend the words. In my mind, I was repeating to myself, HE HIT ME! He's my husband. I thought he would protect me. You would think at that very moment I would have realized I'd married into a family where true happiness was secondary to the opinions of others. Public image mattered in an unhealthy, abnormal way and this family would discredit anyone to keep that image intact.

The doorbell buzzed. All eyes looked to me. The police had arrived. I looked at my husband: his face was filled with terror. Guilt set in for me. I felt the need to protect him. He'd gotten upset, extremely upset. Did one act of rage make him a horrible person? Surely it would never happen again. I'd known Kyle for almost two years and he'd never been physically abusive. Perhaps it was a mistake and he really was sorry.

"No officer, he did not hit me. We had an argument and I called the police because I was upset. It was just a misunderstanding." I recited the rehearsed script robotically. The look on the police officer's face confirmed he did not believe me. He told me that without my statement there would be little that law enforcement could do to prevent a similar incident from occurring again. I assured the officer that I was okay. After he secured witness statements and finished his investigation, I grabbed my baby, went into the bedroom and locked the door to prevent anyone from coming in. I was violated by my husband and unsure of whether he would hit me again as a consequence of calling the police. I needed some time alone to process the events that had just taken place. I finally fell asleep holding my baby in my arms.

We slept for a few hours that seemed like days of rest. I was hoping it would ease the pain of what I had endured. I couldn't understand why I was feeling guilty. I regretted calling the police. Rather than viewing the phone call to the police as a necessary act of protection, I instead felt I had done something terribly wrong.

To add insult to injury, the 'simple misunderstanding' script we rehearsed prior to the arrival of the police had been revised. My mother-in-law gave a witness statement indicating she was present during the altercation. According to her, the incident was solely my fault.

I was completely shocked and I felt betrayed. I wondered if I'd made a mistake by getting married. We hadn't been married a full year and there were already signs of trouble. Yet, I believed it was too soon to give up on our union. I took ownership of Kyle's problem and began brainstorming ways to resolve the conflict. People can get help if they're physically abusive. Perhaps the solution would be to go to counseling with him.

I replayed the events repeatedly in my mind. Subconsciously, I began to doubt myself and wonder if I indeed triggered Kyle's anger and the domestic abuse. I eventually resolved that both my husband and my mother-in-law were right. I had to let it go. To do otherwise would only create more problems. In an attempt to be strong and make the marriage work, I decided to stay. I would forgive this first act of domestic abuse and view it as an isolated incident. I promised myself that if he ever hit me again I would absolutely leave. It was the first of many times that I would recite that same promise.

A few days later, Kyle casually stated in a text message that he would never allow himself to get that angry again. I read the message but did not respond. I wasn't sure if this was his version of an apology. He never actually said the words "I'm sorry." Though I'd been consumed with how to make the situation better, we did not discuss it as a couple. Rather than admit there was a problem, we both operated as if the incident never happened.

After a few weeks of tension, things slowly started to return to normal. In his efforts to regain my trust, he bought me expensive gifts and a brand new luxury car. We took lavish vacations. He befriended everyone in my friendship circle and constantly reminded them of the nice things he did for me. Kyle was charming and created the perfect persona for himself. He needed everyone around us to believe that he was a wonderful person, without flaws. It was the process of convincing people that he was incapable of abusing me before they were even aware of domestic violence.

*****

Three years passed and the joy of motherhood was still a natural high for me. I wanted that experience again. I wanted another baby. Kyle was doing well in his career and figured if a second child would satisfy me then so be it. We soon welcomed another baby boy into our home. I was blessed beyond measure. Motherhood truly is life's most precious gift.

The love that my children brought into my life made it easy to disregard the fact that Kyle and I were slowly drifting apart. He spent the majority of his time at work. I spent all of my time with the children. When Kyle requested that we go to dinner or do things as a couple, I instantly declined. I was consumed with motherhood and showed little interest in doing any activity as a couple. Being a wife was secondary, which furthered the divide within our marriage.

The years that followed proved what I already knew to be true: if you don't get to the root of a problem and address it, the problem will continue to manifest itself. For a while Kyle was able to keep his promise. He was not physically abusive. I felt good about that fact and hopeful for our marriage. I couldn't stomach the thought of being in a relationship where every time there was a disagreement I feared being physically assaulted. However, in the place of physical abuse, I found myself being subjected to emotional abuse and those scars ran deep.

As a result, there were numerous times I packed my bags and left, children in tow. I thought that if I left home enough times Kyle would stop disrespecting me. I hoped he would miss my presence and work harder to address our marital problems. My actions had the opposite effect. Kyle began to make jokes during arguments that suggested I should leave and go to a hotel. He told me how much better he slept when I wasn't at home and that he wished we could live separately forever. I didn't blame him at all for his behavior. Instead, I blamed myself and questioned what I had done to warrant this treatment.

It would be years later before Kyle physically harmed me again. Yet, emotionally, I was in for a roller coaster ride that no one could have prepared me for. If it's true that your hardest times reveal your character, mine was about to be tried, tested and revealed for the world to see.

*****

"You're insecure! That's your problem," he yelled as he stormed upstairs. We were arguing about Dana again. This particular evening, I'd heard the garage door open. His vehicle pulled into the garage, but he didn't come inside the house until well over an hour had passed. He remained in the car conversing with Dana.

The fact that I felt his relationship with Dana was disrespectful was somehow my fault as well. He masked his wrongdoings in condescending remarks aimed at making me feel inferior.

"You never question a man who takes care of his household. Most women do as they're told when a man is providing for them." Didn't I know that? No, I didn't know that because I was stupid. If only I were older, maybe then I would understand. Marrying me was a big mistake. He would talk to anyone he chose to talk to, male or female, at any time. And, that was that.

Their relationship planted the seed of distrust that continued to grow in our marriage. It was a battle between female intuition and my desire to have faith in Kyle. I certainly didn't want to appear immature or insecure. In an effort to prove that neither was the case, I vowed to never question him about his relationship with Dana. I knew that I had no control over his actions.

We never discussed Dana again and I never offered forgiveness. I also didn't leave. I stayed with a hardened heart that would refuse to be mended.

Chapter 2
WELCOME TO CAMPUS LIFE

"Nearly all men can stand adversity, but if you want to test a man's character, give him power."

~ Abraham Lincoln

I remember the beautiful weather when we landed in Kansas. It was my first visit to the state. I didn't know then how much of an impact this brief trip would have on my life.

Kyle was a finalist in the position as president of a public university in Kansas. Our visit was in connection with the presidential search. The three-day agenda was packed with interviews and meetings. We met university faculty, staff, students, constituents, community leaders, politicians, church clergy and the list goes on. The introductions were endless and the questions many. What would be our platform for the university? How efficient would our fundraising initiatives be? How would we position the university for continued growth? Did we understand the challenges of historically black colleges and universities? Did we fully appreciate the nature and pressures of the role of a president and first lady of the university? We answered affirmatively and in solidarity. We were committed. We understood the challenges. We were a team.

The opportunity to meet university stakeholders was the most gratifying part of the campus visit. We spent a substantial amount of time with the interim president of the university who reminded me of my paternal grandfather. He was very gracious and wise. His love for the university was contagious. He spoke of its history and culture in a way that instantly caused me to share his passion.

Our assigned campus guide was equally kind and informative. He provided encouragement between each interview session. As we were leaving the campus, a recent graduate expressed to me that the university operated like a family. I instantly concurred. In a short amount of time, it was apparent that the people we met possessed a deep love for the institution and had a vested interest in its success.

Two days later, we received an announcement that Kyle was selected to be the next president of the university. It would be his first time serving in that capacity. I couldn't have been happier for him. His lifelong dream of being a college president was finally being fulfilled. It was a wonderful time for our family.

After the celebration, days of relocation planning followed. Since marriage, I had become what was popularly referenced among higher education professionals as the trailing spouse, terminology used to describe a situation where one spouse is required to relocate as a result of their companion acquiring a new job assignment. Consequently, the trailing spouse faces a range of issues that impact them personally and professionally.

The impending relocation from Michigan to Kansas would represent the third move for me within our six years of marriage. As an attorney, each transition required me to obtain admission to practice law by taking a bar examination in the various states in which we lived. Kyle never acknowledged any of my personal sacrifices. Once again, I would be required to put aside my employment, friendship ties and established networks in pursuit of Kyle's career progression. I wanted to be a supportive wife, but it certainly wasn't easy. The move would be a major adjustment for our entire family.

I hoped the move to Kansas would represent a fresh start for us. Things were going fairly well by this time. I'd blocked out of my mind that Kyle had been physically and emotionally abusive. I didn't dwell on whether or not there were any acts of infidelity. I wanted us to be a normal, happy family.

*****

Welcome to campus life! We were eager to get settled and acclimated to Kansas. It was an immediate lifestyle change. Our new home was directly in the center of the campus. I looked out the windows and saw the student union, student housing, classroom buildings and university offices. Though it was owned by the university, it was now our home as long as Kyle retained the position of president. It was spacious with plenty of room for the children to play. There was a large entertainment area in the basement where we hosted meetings, luncheons and other events.

The first few months were intense. There was a huge learning curve for Kyle as he adjusted to his new position. His workdays were extremely long. His travel increased, so prolonged periods of time away from home became the norm. We quickly adjusted to busy and hectic as our new standard of living.

Before the move to Kansas, I was working as an attorney in the legal affairs office on a university campus. This experience provided insight into the myriad of issues that college campuses face, the politics at play in decision making, risk management concerns and student life. When we relocated, we decided that rather than me seeking employment in a legal capacity, I would become actively engaged on the campus. There hadn't been a first lady on this campus for years, so there was great latitude given in defining what the role should be.

To gain a deeper understanding of the parameters of my role, I connected with other university spouses through professional organizations such as the American Association of State Colleges and Universities. They had a program specifically designed for spouses of university presidents. I also spoke with university stakeholders and completed a campus survey to get the input of students to assess the needs of the campus.

I wanted to help make the campus experience engaging and fun. I served on various committees to understand the framework before I transitioned into being an event planner and hostess for campus functions. My attention to detail proved to be helpful when I organized events. I worked closely with the campus staff to ensure that the activities and programs went off without a hitch.

In alignment with my passion, I implemented a Pre-Law Society to afford aspiring young attorneys insight and exposure to the possibilities a law degree could offer. I hosted an annual dinner to connect female students with professionals in leadership positions which allowed for effective dialogue and discussion. I organized social activities: ice cream socials, clothing swaps, community service projects in partnership with the sororities and campus organizations. Our children attended the university daycare, which helped me to become actively engaged with that facet of the campus as well. I often advised females who struggled to find a comfortable balance between parenting responsibilities and the demands of being a college student.

I worked in conjunction with the university's development office to explore fundraising ideas that would sustain additional programming. This collaboration aided in identifying female alumnae who shared a passion for female empowerment. An annual leadership luncheon was instituted that led way to a renewed interest in the overall wellbeing of female students attending the university.

My position later evolved to include any and all programming that would garner support for female students and the challenges they faced. The objective was to provide mentors and position them to successfully achieve their goals. I was excited about this endeavor because I was afforded the same level of support throughout my matriculation in both undergraduate and graduate studies. As a result, I recognized the importance of positive role models and dedicated mentors. I knew that it absolutely mattered.

Through a partnership with a national community service organization, we formalized a campus mentoring program. This was key in further solidifying efforts to support our female students. Workshops and seminars were offered that included topics in the areas of professional development, personal image, etiquette and self-esteem.

Student engagement was paramount in my new role and I embraced each opportunity to have interaction with the students. Helping them to become the best version of themselves forced me to examine the areas in my life that needed improvement.

*****

In addition to my work as first lady, there were joint spousal duties that required my attention. University fundraising was at the top of the list. It was no secret that this was the least favorite of my activities. However, I quickly brainstormed ways to be instrumental in the success of those initiatives and later developed a plan that became the framework for Kyle's annual fundraising campaign.

As with most relocations, there were many changes that occurred immediately. Within the first few months, I gained a deeper understanding of the presidential role and its accompanying demands. Yet, there was one challenge I had not prepared for: the presidential ego. The shift in attitude that came from Kyle's newfound sense of perceived power and control brought destruction once again to our household.

Chapter 3
PRIVATE LIFE VS. PUBLIC LIES

Narcissistic personality disorder is defined as a condition in which people have an excessive sense of self-importance, and extreme preoccupation with themselves, and lack of empathy for others.

"Your husband sounds like a narcissist," the counselor said. I had been regularly engaged in counseling for the past few months. I made the decision to see a counselor to sort through the frustrations I felt within the marriage. Naively, I thought the move to Kansas would strengthen our family. The reality was the marriage was still in shambles.

I'd spent the past hour talking to the counselor about how things progressed. It felt good to say what I was feeling out loud to someone with the protection of confidentiality. I suffered emotionally as a result of keeping those feelings bottled inside of me for so many years. I was disappointed in myself for remaining in a relationship with someone who physically abused me. Additionally, as a result of the continual emotional abuse my self-esteem was at an all time low.

Publicly, we were the perfect couple. Kyle stood up at events and spewed out praises to me for being a supportive wife and loving mother. Behind closed doors the physical abuse escalated. I avoided confrontation because I knew any argument would lead to abuse. We resorted to communicating either through text message or by way of emails from his secretary. We didn't operate as though we were married. There wasn't even a friendship left. However, Kyle wanted the marriage to stay intact because it was good for his image. "The campus loves the idea of a family as the presidential unit, and that's what we will give them," he often stated.

As campus administrators, we were quickly elevated to a position of being role models for thousands of college students and leaders within the community. Our children were affectionately called the little lions of the campus, in reference to the school's mascot. Consequently, Kyle critiqued everything about me in his effort to craft how he wanted us to be received on the campus. He developed a sense of paranoia and expressed that we could no longer lead normal lives.

It became fairly obvious to me that the pressures of being liked and conforming to the public image Kyle created was consuming him. He was self-absorbed, out of touch and regarded himself as among the social elite. His focus was solely on his career. Any other conversation, especially concerning our family or the marriage, was annoying to him.

His idea of transformative leadership was rapidly showing signs of dictatorship. We disagreed on almost everything, which ultimately led to us discussing nothing. Kyle's communication with me was always condescending, filled with disdain and violent patriarchy. He reminded me that I should feel fortunate to be married to him, and assured me that I could be replaced at any time: "You ungrateful, immature bitch! I work my ass off every day so that you and the kids can enjoy this lifestyle. Any other woman would love to be in your position!"

My mechanism for dealing with problems hadn't changed. I avoided issues and potential conflict. Staying busy was easy to do. At home, I was going through the "Married-Single Parent Dilemma". Kyle had become an absent parent consumed with the roles, responsibilities and challenges of his new job. Even when he wasn't traveling, he spent extended periods of time at his office or attending work-related events. This left me responsible for all household duties and everything involving the children.

We had done very little in the way of rebuilding the trust between us. Questions of infidelity rose again. Rumors of a student on the campus being pregnant by Kyle surfaced. Later, there was speculation of an inappropriate relationship between Kyle and a university administrator. I was constantly bombarded with information that caused me to question his integrity. It became hard to decipher what was gossip with what was factual. I found myself in a state of unhappiness. It was a train wreck waiting to happen.

Discernment became paramount in our new leadership

roles at the university. My email was flooded with people who wanted to meet for breakfast, lunch, dinner and all times in between. I was invited to more banquets, galas, fundraisers, and events than I could ever hope to attend. There was no shortage of human bodies present in our circle. Yet, I still felt as though there was no one to talk to. During conversations with university constituents, Kyle engaged superficially about how the family enjoyed Kansas and more directly on university issues. He constantly reminded me that I would never understand the intricate relationships and everyone's indirect tie to the university. His controlling personality also dictated who my friends were. He was suspicious about me creating friendships and often cautioned against it. "We are considered outsiders because we are not from Kansas. Trust no one."

It was true that most of our colleagues were natives of the state and had a much deeper sense of the history and operations of the university. This was the basis for his rationale as to why I should neither feel supported by nor comfortable forming friendships with anyone.

As a result, I refrained from any discussion of personal matters. Could anyone fully comprehend the dynamics of what I was experiencing? Not likely. I concluded that I would either be viewed as complaining about living a luxurious lifestyle in a presidential home funded by the university or I would receive the standard "I understand" feedback. The reality was no one had a clue as to the magnitude of our situation and we worked harder to keep it that way.

Most days I was completely exhausted but I couldn't let my fatigue show. The public performance and façade was a requirement. Prior to any event, Kyle reviewed what his expectations of me were. The tone of the conversation was similar to that of a parent giving forewarning to a child: you will listen and obey, or you will pay a price for your disobedience. The price that I paid was almost always in the form of abuse. As long as I performed well in our public life, there was no concern for what was consuming me privately. I was to do as I was told, and with a smile.

The physical abuse had initially been sporadic. Now, the exchanges were bitter most times ending with a push, slap or punch. I still felt an obligation to protect him even when he physically abused me. I didn't want anything bad to happen to him. All I wanted was for the abuse and constant disrespect to cease.

The emotional strain was enormous. However, I didn't have the luxury to stop and deal with it. Life was busy. Moments after being emotionally abused or harmed physically, I was off to the next campus event as if nothing ever happened.

I often walked into campus activities just moments after crying. I kept makeup in my purse that helped to conceal evidence of my tears. I would learn the hard way that makeup, jewelry and expensive clothing should never be used to cover up your pain.

*****

I was a guest speaker on a leadership panel. The auditorium was filled with young students with blank slates. I wanted them to get life right the first time around. Learn from the mistakes of others. "Be authentic," I proclaimed. "Never sacrifice your self-worth. Assume responsibility for your actions." I was giving sound advice and pouring knowledge into others to deflect from the reality of my own pain. My physical appearance looked amazing though my spirit was slowly dying. I was pouring from an empty cup. I had not taken the time to nurture my emotional health. Private life versus public lies... it was slowly taking a toll on me.

*****

I remember playing a game called MASH in middle school with my friends. It was a game used to predict our future. MASH was an acronym for Mansion, Apartment, Shack or Home. There were various categories in this game, including who you would marry, how many kids you would have, the kind of car you would drive, what your profession would be, where you would live, and so many other life determinations. The items that remained under each category at the completion of the game were considered to define your future.

It was a popular game that we played often. We were innocent little girls, dreaming of fairytale weddings with the perfect husband. Romanticizing the notion of marriage continued through our high school years. We fantasized about wedding dresses and honeymoon locations. In our minds, being married wasn't optional. It was one of the items to check off your list if you considered yourself successful.

By the age of 25, I'd found what most would consider a good man by modern day societal standards. Kyle was a well-educated black man, on the rise in his professional career. He was an eligible bachelor who happened to be 12 years older than me. He was charismatic and charming. He hardly ever met a stranger. Kyle had been married before and had children from his previous marriage. He purported to be a single parent who was committed to family values.

Had Kyle been listed as a marriage option during my youthful days of playing MASH, he certainly would have been one of my top picks. He seemed to possess all of the characteristics I desired in a husband. On top of being everything I'd dreamed of, he was also able to financially provide a comfortable lifestyle for our family. We dated and were engaged in less than a year. I was confident we would spend the rest of our lives together.

I later learned that the person Kyle portrayed himself to be publicly was in stark contrast to the person he was privately. Out in the open, he was loving, kind and appeared genuinely concerned for the wellbeing of others. Behind closed doors he was a control freak and only cared about what made him look good publicly. He would go to any extreme for his career and he was willing to sacrifice anything or anyone in the process.

Any form of disagreement with Kyle led to name-calling and attempts to destroy my self-esteem. His way was the only way. He manipulated who our family friends were by his perception of their importance. If a relationship with them could benefit Kyle, then we could maintain a friendship. Otherwise, he considered the friendship useless.

I noticed these signs of controlling behavior early on in the marriage. I attributed our differences of opinion to the age span between us. Later, I excused his behavior under the assumption that he was dealing with the stress of his new job. It was hard for me to accept the fact that a marriage that was just getting started was already failing. That wasn't my idea of happily ever after.

Creating what we thought was the perfect marriage also meant that I couldn't let anyone know the truth of what was going on. I wondered if people could sense our problems when we were out in public. It was shameful and horrifying. Everyone was applauding us for being young, successful, doting new parents and the ideal married couple. How could I now admit that he was abusive and that our fairytale life was a lie?

I continued to pray that it would never happen again. I told myself that every incident was the last time. When we argued, I tried to ensure it didn't escalate to the point of physical contact. I thought I actually had control over that. The only real control that I had was removing myself from the situation, but I didn't and the abuse continued.

The emotional abuse was harder to deal with than the physical abuse. At times I didn't appreciate or understand the level of manipulation being used, although it surfaced in every conversation we had. Rather than finding value in my employment or achievements, Kyle referred to any success as a byproduct of his professional status. "If you leave me, I'll ensure you have nothing. You can't survive without me. I provide for this family. Do you know how stupid you would look if you left me? Everyone will think that you're crazy! You are crazy!" Kyle would make similar comments regarding everything we acquired together during the marriage: "You never lived like this until you married me! You won't be anything without me!"

Kyle's attitude became increasingly worse. His ego seemed

to control every situation. His constant reminder that I somehow lived a good life because of him was growing old. Nothing was really good about our life. It was not genuine. We were frauds. We portrayed a perfect lifestyle and lived in direct opposition to the public image we presented. I was conflicted by our public image. I knew the real Kyle. The person who constantly disrespected and abused me. I was privy to our truth and burdened by the weight of hiding our reality. Was that a good life? Not by my standards.

I allowed myself to believe that I wasn't affected by anything he said. Yet, my inaction indicated otherwise. I stayed. I devalued myself. There was no denying that truth.

*****

Once Kyle was in a leadership position, I noticed the same behaviors he exhibited in the marriage surface in his career decisions. I became mindful of how he treated his subordinates and his lack of integrity in his professional relationships. He ranked his staff by level of importance and often shunned those he felt were beneath him.

"You're so fake!" I was yelling again. We were in the middle of another one of many arguments, which began when Kyle scolded me about my friendship with the wife of an administrator. Angel lived closed to us on the campus. We would get together for walks in the evenings to debrief on campus activities and events. On this particular evening, I invited her to our home. After a few hours of chatting and letting our children play together, she left. Within seconds of her departure, Kyle arrived and instantly began screaming at me. "You should be careful who you let come over to this house! You're so naïve. You don't understand the political landscape. Every decision is a political decision. I have told you before it is not acceptable for employees of the university or their spouses to be at this house unless it's for a university event. You have invited Angel into the house and you have no idea I'm about to fire her husband. Your stupid decisions constantly make my job hard! Don't have anyone over here without asking me first!"

I wasn't happy that I had to endure another one of Kyle's paranoid selection processes of determining who our friends should be. According to him, everyone was envious of him and his position, so I should only communicate with those people on his approved list. I was very confused because he knew that Angel and I were friends. However, he seemed to be very concerned that she was at our home. I was disturbed because I had no reason to believe that he was unhappy with the job performance of Angel's husband. Kyle recruited Angel's family to the university. He sold them on his leadership and promised to be a source of support to them. Only a few months had passed and Kyle was ready to terminate him.

I snapped back at Kyle's attempt to scold me.

"Why would you want to fire him when you're the reason why he's here? You hired him!" I said.

"Because he's young," Kyle responded. "He's young and I'm tired of having to micromanage his department. I trusted the advice of a friend when hiring him. In actuality, I shouldn't have given him a chance. He was almost fired from his previous job. He doesn't handle responsibility well. He claims he works late hours but nothing gets done. He's simply not ready for this position. He was advanced too soon and does not fit well with my leadership style. I'm terminating him and moving in a different direction."

I became more upset with every word that he said.

Hypocrite! Fraud! My resentment for him was turning to hatred. Had Kyle forgotten that when he applied for president at this university, he was labeled as being too young? Why didn't he feel an obligation to be a mentor to this administrator rather than talk about him behind his back? I'd watched as Kyle smiled in his face at every possible opportunity. Yet, at the first hint of disagreement, Kyle was ready to cut him off. I felt it was an unprofessional way to handle the situation. Additionally, I wasn't pleased that my friendship with Angel was being dictated by who Kyle felt was important in the moment.

I shouldn't have been surprised because this had become

Kyle's pattern of establishing relationships solely based on what the other person could offer him. Kyle created his success by strategically forming the right relationships, essentially being an opportunist. He was extremely judgmental of everyone but found no fault with himself. There was no such thing as constructive criticism when it came to Kyle. He would constantly surround himself with 'yes men,' those who supported his opinions and ideas with little or no criticism in order to obtain his approval. It was not uncommon for Kyle to retaliate against his subordinates if they expressed dissent or opposing views. His employees knew that either you agreed with him or you would find yourself on the chopping block at risk of being terminated.

I was shocked by Kyle's transformation. He made fiscal and managerial decisions that could have easily led to a legal nightmare for him and the university. I wanted to offer guidance to him, particularly with my background in defending lawsuits for another university. I knew that Kyle would need an understanding of all of the rules applicable to higher education law. However, I wouldn't dare caution him when I felt he was making a mistake. Kyle was not interested in my opinion or advice. He operated the university in the manner in which he felt was best, without fear of any consequence for his actions.

Kyle made the decision to mix university business with personal pleasure. He relocated Olivia, an old girlfriend, to

Kansas and hired her for an open position at the university. Their history spanned back to their times as undergraduates in college. They later began dating and lived together during their graduate studies.

Kyle did not mention to me that Olivia was a candidate for the position, on campus for an interview, or selected for the job. When I glanced through my university email, I saw the announcement of a new administrator. My jaw dropped. It took me a few minutes to process what I had just read. I assured myself Kyle would not be that disrespectful. No one could possibly be that disrespectful. This must be a different person. Although I knew I was correct. The picture of her displayed in the congratulatory email message certainly solidified her identity.

I picked up the telephone. I don't remember dialing the numbers to Kyle's office, but I now heard Linda, his assistant, on the other end of the line: "Office of the President." He was in a meeting.
"Should he be interrupted?" Linda asked.
"Yes, absolutely."
"Can you state the nature of the call?"
"No. It's personal, very personal."

Kyle responded angrily to my inquiry about Olivia: "Don't call my office with this bullshit! Yes, Olivia got the job. I don't have to tell you every decision I make on this campus."

"I'm not interested in every decision you make, arrogant asshole!" I screamed back. "I'm interested in the fact that you hired Olivia on this campus and didn't even give me the courtesy of a heads up. That's a decision I want to know about!"

I was fuming and Kyle was still screaming into the phone. I abruptly interrupted his rant as I hung up the phone.

The manner in which Kyle hired Olivia was a blatant form of disrespect. I was extremely hurt and was no longer excited about supporting Kyle's initiatives at the university. I decided to resign from the campus committees I served on and shifted my focus to my children and my career.

*****

Linda shared a very close relationship with Kyle and he often stated it was because she was loyal. For Kyle, that simply meant that Linda was his puppet and responded accordingly. She did exactly as she was told and would lie to cover up any of his wrongdoings.

Linda performed tasks of a personal nature for Kyle. When I made the decision to return to work, she was the person who coordinated his schedule and informed me if Kyle would be available to assist with picking the kids up from school. Both Linda and Kyle treated my communication with them as a privilege or honor they were bestowing upon me. If I needed help with the children, I was told to contact Linda and patiently await a response. If there was any time to squeeze in Kyle's busy, demanding, important life as university president, Linda would let me know. Even if I asked Kyle directly to help with the children while he was in my presence, I was directed to contact Linda for his availability. He was much too busy for such trivial things. Linda would filter my requests and make the final determination.

I was perplexed by the fact that I lived in the same house with a man who was my husband, yet we couldn't even discuss matters concerning our children. It was clear that taking care of the children was solely my job. Kyle's job was to be president and receive accolades. That's where he placed his importance. Receiving constant praise fueled his distorted sense of happiness.

*****

The counselor asked what I felt was the underlying issue at play? I wished I had an answer to her question and an accompanying solution to the problem, but the reality was I did not. I did feel strongly that Kyle was dealing with some personal struggles. He had a constant desire to make people feel inferior to him. He wanted to be needed and he thrived off of control. The more control you gave him, the happier he was. Hitting me and demeaning me was just one of many ways he exercised such control.

I'd tried several ways of dealing with Kyle's erratic and violent behavior – from total support of his professional endeavors to complete withdrawal from Kyle and our relationship. Kyle didn't seem to notice either of my methods of handling the situation, and continued his usual course of behavior. As Kyle began to act invincible, I felt more invisible. I was hoping the counselor could offer some professional guidance.

She listened intently and occasionally scribbled some notes on her notepad. "Narcissists are hard to deal with in a position of power," she whispered, "but I can give you some coping mechanisms."

At a subsequent counseling session, I arrived ready to once again discuss my discontent and frustration. Before I could start down that path, the counselor posed the following questions: "What are you holding onto that you need to release? Are you resentful and angry? If you feel you deserve better, what actions will you take? Let's shift the focus to you and what you can control. You can no longer remain idle. Your situation will not change unless you change it." She was advising me that a shift in mindset would be a necessary prerequisite to developing a plan to move forward.

Chapter 4
SHOWTIME!

"It's like you're a character in this book that everyone around you is writing, and suddenly you have to say, 'I'm sorry, but this role isn't right for me'. And you have to start writing your own life and doing your own thing."
~ David Levithan

Neither I nor Kyle was prepared for an unexpected life change. When I became pregnant with our third child, Kyle was furious. He felt it would hinder his ability to continue advancing in his career and that the added responsibility would decrease the level of support I would be able to offer to him.

Knowing that Kyle didn't want our baby was the point where I lost all hope for our marriage. I was disgusted with the man I had married. I listened as he gave public speeches about being happy for our growing family only to return home to him screaming and yelling at me for being pregnant.

"Another pregnancy was the last thing we needed. How can you be any help with fundraising and other university activities if you're pregnant? This job requires frequent travel and financial donors expect to see both of us. We should be making connections. Instead, you'll be home sick and pregnant. Since you trapped me by getting pregnant, you'll be forced to do everything on your own, without any support from me. You knew that I was busy before you decided to keep the baby! You should have had an abortion!"

I was humiliated. Our marriage was broken, but I was still his wife. Who talked to their wife in that manner? What did he mean by saying he was being trapped by a pregnancy? How could he utter the word abortion? I was suffering from depression. In my mind, this was my karma. All of the emotions that I felt years prior when making the decision to have an abortion began to resurface. There was no way I would go through the horrific experience of terminating a pregnancy again.

During one argument, Kyle pushed me down several flights of stairs in our home. When he rushed down to where I'd fallen, I expected some form of care, concern, regret and maybe even an apology. I received neither. Kyle responded by saying he hoped the fall would result in me losing the baby.

Kyle had not attended a single prenatal doctor's appointment with me during the pregnancy. I drove myself to the hospital that afternoon. When I arrived, I told the doctor that I slipped and had fallen down the stairs and I wanted to make sure the baby had not been harmed. The ultrasound revealed that the baby was doing well. When I left the hospital I said a prayer. Once I made it through this pregnancy, I was leaving Kansas. I could not forgive Kyle again.

A few months later, I gave birth to our third child. Not much changed. Kyle began sleeping on the sofa downstairs and I slept in our bedroom upstairs. I don't recall how it happened. I never actually told him to sleep on the sofa, but I made it obvious I didn't want to be near him. There was no intimacy between us. In fact, it was a welcome reward. Whenever Kyle entered our bedroom, I cringed. He was a guest in our bedroom and my actions let him know it.

Occasionally, we still attended university events but they had certainly become limited and we would always arrive separately. It was very awkward. We would sit at a table and make small talk with guests even though we hadn't uttered a word to each other within the home in weeks. A few times, we even answered questions posed to us differently and would have to cover up the reality that we were literally strangers to each other. Kyle knew very little of what was going on in my world and vice versa.

*****

It was homecoming month, one of the busiest and most exciting times on campus. For me, it also meant being obligated to attend homecoming festivities and pretend our marriage wasn't merely a charade. The annual homecoming gala that year was no different. I arrived to the gala an hour after Kyle. He greeted me when I entered and gave me a quick overview of the people who would be seated at our table. As I received my instructions for the night, we casually smiled and waved to guests. We were each doing what we needed to do in order to get through the moment with the least amount of scrutiny. It was standard practice in our business deal of a marriage: Thanks for showing up as my business partner in this venture. Here's a list of key donors. Entertain them well and you'll be compensated. Remember, any other person would love to have your position so you should be honored to be in attendance with me. You should do as I say. Your opinion is whatever I say it is.

That's where we were in the relationship at that point. I would remain silent, smile and hope that the time spent together passed quickly.

Things were going smoothly the night of the homecoming gala. We each wore our fake smiles we'd grown accustomed to wearing. We sat together and entertained the university donors in hopes that the end result would be a huge check to the university. I applauded Kyle's efforts as president. He acknowledged my role as a supportive wife. We outlined the strategic plans for the university and our excitement for the future. The recitation included enrollment and retention data, financial projections and the quality of customer service being offered to the students. The conversation was so standard and routine I could probably repeat the talking points in my sleep.

Finally, the gala was over. I was preparing to make a dash to the nearest exit when a photographer requested to take our photo. I kindly refused. I had done my part. I survived the night and played my role extremely well. I could now retreat back to the safety of my bedroom and the comfort of my children.

I had no idea that my refusal to take the photograph made Kyle angry. I had been home for almost two hours before he returned. He entered cursing and screaming. I begged him to calm down for fear that he would wake the children. Kyle refused to lower his voice.

"Crazy bitch! This is my job on the line. I've worked all of my life to be here and I'll be damned if I let you ruin it."

As I walked away from him, he hit me. "I told you that I would never let you put your hands on me again!" I yelled. "This is the last time!"

Sadly, it had been the last time numerous times before. At this point, my threats had little meaning to Kyle. As he continued in his rage, I knew I had to stop him. I called the police department for the city and was informed that because we lived on campus, the university police had jurisdiction. I felt hopeless. The university police department worked for Kyle. I didn't need university police to come to our residence for a domestic dispute involving the university's president! That would be a major conflict of interest. I needed someone from the local police department to respond immediately. The dispatcher apologized for not being able to help me and then transferred the call to the campus police.

Minutes later, the chief of police arrived at the home. It was no surprise that Tom and Kyle were friends. Kyle hired Tom and was his direct supervisor. I was not hopeful that my complaint would be taken seriously and my concern was valid. Tom parked discreetly on the side of the house in an unmarked vehicle and sat downstairs talking to Kyle for over an hour. They engaged in conversation, laughed and at one point I even heard Kyle offer Tom something to drink. You would have thought we invited Tom over for dinner rather than for a case of domestic violence.

When Tom finally came upstairs to talk to me, he did not ask what happened. He clearly was not interested in investigating domestic abuse. He simply stated that Kyle was sorry and it wouldn't happen again. Tom suggested that we both get some rest. He told me that he would make sure word of this incident did not get out in the community. In his opinion, that was the last thing we needed.

I'd certainly heard that line before. We didn't need other people in our marital affairs. Everyone seemed to be of the mindset that domestic violence would solve itself as long as it wasn't discussed.

I was terrified. Kyle showed no remorse after any incidents of abuse and each instance was getting progressively worse. I knew that he would be physically abusive again after being assured that the university police chief would ignore my plea for help. Kyle operated as if it validated what he'd told me all along: You are here because of me. You will either do what I say or be destroyed.

Our next encounter with the university police department was a result of my plan to separate from Kyle and leave the university residence. I was hopeful that a long overdue conversation with Kyle would be a positive step toward resolution of our problems. I calmly spoke with Kyle about the fact that I was unhappy and had been unhappy for quite some time. I explained that I could not continue to allow him to hit me and also how his actions were affecting me. I was also concerned for the kids. Even though they were young I didn't want them to grow up thinking that abusive behavior was okay. I planned to take the children with me to stay with family in Louisiana and give our marriage a break. Maybe the time apart would be good for both of us.

Kyle interrupted me: "You will not take the children anywhere! Is this your way of seeking revenge? Besides, no one will believe anything you say about me. I will not let you make a fool out of me."

It was clear that I would not get through to him. Every issue revolved around how it would make him look publicly. My attempts at communication with him failed.

As I reached to get our youngest child from Kyle, he shoved me onto the living room floor. I remained on the floor and cried uncontrollably. I kept telling myself to get up and get the children. It's time to leave. I realized that as a result of my screaming, the baby was also crying. I gathered the energy to comfort the baby, but not before I heard Kyle on the phone with Tom. "Come over here. She's acting crazy and threatening to leave me."

In Kyle's opinion, any awareness of domestic abuse could put his job in jeopardy. Consequently, he made it clear to the campus police officers that I was the enemy and should be treated as such. Kyle directed Tom to follow me around campus and report back to him regarding anyone I was meeting with or talking to. Tom became personally invested in our marital problems. He and other officers issued verbal threats to me indicating I would get what I deserved. It became a horrific nightmare.

Kyle's goal was to make me feel broken and helpless so that I had no choice but to allow the control to continue. Though I grew weary of defending myself and our marriage, I was gaining strength at my weakest point. As much as I didn't want the marriage to be a failure, I knew that I couldn't continue to raise our children in the midst of chaos. I also would not be able to continue to force a public smile in support of someone who did not respect me. In a state of brokenness, I developed the courage I would need to later walk away. I didn't even know that was possible. It's true that your purpose can be manifested through your pain.

*****

I'd been coping for the last year and a half but recognized that our life was a performance. When it was show time, I was on and did what I felt were my wifely duties to show extreme support. However, it was evident to those closest to us that a break up was on the horizon. I'm not sure if Kyle noticed because he was very busy in his position, or at least enjoying the title that came along with the position: 'Mr. President.' He was basking in its superficial glow.

There was talk of marital affairs and campus constituencies approached me constantly in that regard. At this point, infidelity was the least of my concerns: physical intimacy had not been a priority for several months. However, when the opportunity for retaliation presented itself, I quickly stepped up to the plate. The campus wanted to know if there was any truth to the rumors about Olivia and Kyle. Was Olivia really Kyle's new mistress? I responded factually and affirmatively. Hurt people hurt people. I was slowly becoming the person who had hurt me.

I was certainly not surprised that Kyle would take offense to the statements I'd made. I'd also grown accustomed to his rants of anger. "I fucking hate you! I had a member of my governing board to ask me about this bullshit! Do you understand how serious that is? Do you realize this job provides for you? You are crazy!"

Crazy?! No, I'm not crazy. I married crazy! I thought to myself. That was his new label for me. Anytime I acted contrary to his wishes, surely I must be crazy. If I didn't engage in the right conversations, I was crazy. If I asked him to assist me in caring for the kids, I clearly didn't understand the demands of his job as a university president and was therefore crazy.

Blah, I had heard it all numerous times before. With each affirmation of his despisal for me, the words had less of an impact. It was late and I was tired. I had been asleep when Kyle burst into the bedroom. It startled me and I wondered why he was even there. I didn't have the energy for an argument. Please just go back to the sofa where you've been sleeping, I thought. As he cursed at me, I sat up, looked him directly in his eyes and calmly said, "Stop screaming. I don't care about you. As a matter of fact, I hate you, too! You have completely ruined my life. Now, please shut the door on your way out."

TIFFANY HILL

Chapter 5
HOMOPHOBIA

Merriam Webster dictionary defines homophobia as an irrational fear of, aversion to, or discrimination against homosexuality or homosexuals. The person who exhibits this behavior is referred to as a homophobe.

*****

You've covered your face with a heterosexual mask,

buried your homophobic truth in

infidelity, insecurity and lies;

masking who you are to conform

to who the world wants you to be;

You chose to surround me only with those

who held titles befitting enough to be in your presence.

To simply be silent and controlled

was your desire for me.

You failed to comprehend

that you can neither control that

which you do not own,

nor demand submission without

being deserving of it.

The lack of respect ran deep both ways.

I viewed you as an animal that would

devour anything in its path.

Your perspective of me was less than,

AUTHENTIC ME

unworthy of and subordinate to you.

You boasted often of the joy you stole from

your previous wife, viewing yourself as superior

while she remained inferior; yet you call yourself a man.

I could no longer view you as such.

A little boy you are, trapped inside a man's body.

An adult by way of age only,

searching for wholeness.

Your Catholic upbringing masks

family secrets and dark stories,

rooted so deep that you're

unsure of your own truth.

I couldn't be unapologetically me

because we were too busy

being un-authentically you.

I was crazy because I was a part of you,

Intertwined yet unaware that

your crazy was now me.

I laid with you, I stood beside you,

I cried for you when you were too

arrogant to cry for your damn self...

My heart let go of crazy.

What I once was I am no more.

I grew up in the south: in a small town in the state of Louisiana. I was an 80's baby. Being gay was not generally accepted. Prayer was the answer to everything in our Baptist church community. The notion was that if someone somehow mistakenly thought they were homosexual, the church could rally around the person and pray it out of them. To avoid the embarrassment, a person could choose to remain 'in the closet'.

This culture of being ashamed to express your sexuality was pervasive within African American families. It pained me to see people pretend they were heterosexual when they were home with family, and live a different lifestyle when they were with their friends. The lack of authenticity was troubling to me.

*****

"I don't want gay men around me! I don't have a problem with them being gay, but I can't be friends with someone who is gay. They can't be around me and be gay," Kyle stated proudly. This rant about gay men came out of nowhere. I had a friend visiting that weekend who openly identified as being homosexual. I took Kyle's words as an attack on my friend. However, Kyle's comment about gay men was deeper than this surface level conversation. Rather than condemning the gay community because their beliefs were different from his, it seemed he was instead defending himself. Kyle needed me to be clear that he wasn't gay and never would be gay, which was odd because I never questioned his sexuality.

Things later took an interesting turn when homophobia surfaced in the place that I least expected... our marriage.

*****

I was scheduled to be out of town for the entire day to attend meetings. I returned home earlier than expected. As I entered the home, I noticed Kyle's suit coat jacket draped over a chair in the entryway. That was strange. He was hardly ever home and certainly not during the middle of the day. I slowly took off my shoes and left them by the front door. I didn't want the sound of my high heels hitting the floor to alert anyone to the fact that I was there.

Our bedroom area was upstairs. You could either take the stairway or the elevator. I knew that I couldn't take the elevator because the noise as it opened would also let him know I was home.

I rushed up the stairs as quickly and quietly as I could only to find that the door to the stairwell was locked. My heart was racing and I was becoming increasingly upset. Surely Kyle would not have a woman in our home and in my bedroom! It was definitely my bedroom because he hadn't slept there in almost a year. I was convinced that Kyle was cheating on me.

Breathe, relax and calm down! That's what I had to do to think clearly. I realized I was still holding my keys in my hand, which included the key to unlock the door to the stairway. I turned it slowly and began walking down the hall to a closed bedroom door. I swung the door open so hard it hit the wall as I stormed into the bedroom. It was empty. I checked the bathroom. No one was there. I searched all of the bedrooms upstairs and even the closets. They were all empty. I sat down on the edge of the bed. I'd gotten myself upset over nothing. Kyle constantly told me I was insecure. Maybe he was right. I needed to pull it together.

I took the elevator down to get my purse, shoes and other items I had hurriedly dropped at the door. When the elevator chimed on the first level and I walked off, I saw Kyle. Apparently, he heard the noise of the elevator and walked out of the living room. He seemed disheveled and very surprised to see me. When I inquired as to why he was home midday, he quickly stated that he stopped by while walking to a campus meeting because needed to get some papers from his home office. As he was explaining this, Bryan walked out of the living room as well. Now I was a bit confused. Why was Bryan here?

I glanced at them both with a puzzled look. Bryan worked on the campus. He was also a family friend that we'd known for years so it wasn't particularly shocking to see him at our home. What was odd about the situation was the fact that I had walked past the office, by the living room, and through the entire downstairs area to rush upstairs just a few minutes earlier. There weren't any lights on downstairs. I hadn't heard any conversation or noticed anything that would indicate they were there working. I didn't feel there was a reason to doubt what they said, yet their explanation didn't make sense to me.

I wished them well on the rest of their day and rushed back upstairs to change clothes. It would be almost a year later before I would reflect on this day again and understand exactly why something was not quite right about that brief encounter.

*****

Kyle was raised Catholic. I, on the other hand, had never stepped foot inside a Catholic church until I met him. One of our conversations while dating was that I didn't want to attend a Catholic church. I desired to continue going to Baptist churches. Kyle wasn't attending any church regularly and was amenable to joining me at a local Baptist church. He later stated that although he was raised Catholic, he didn't like the Catholic Church and felt they covered up a lot of issues. It was a moment of vulnerability. I sensed that he didn't want to discuss what caused him to denounce his Catholic upbringing as he never told me what the issue was. However, when he visited his family, Kyle eagerly participated in all of the Catholic rituals. On one occasion, I inquired as to whether his disdain for the Catholic religion had anything to do with the allegations regarding sex abuse scandals. Kyle neither answered nor mentioned the Catholic Church again.

Another source of vulnerability for Kyle relating to his childhood was his family. Kyle's father had been an alcoholic, which put a strain on his parents' marriage. His parents often slept in different bedrooms and he rarely saw them show affection towards each other.

I often wondered if that perception of marriage is why Kyle failed at marriages. Initially, I truly believed that Kyle wanted our marriage to work. But when conflict arose, he resorted back to what he had been shown by his own parents: division can run deep behind closed doors, as long as there's never a sign of it publicly.

Early in our marriage, I foolishly thought I could change him. As years passed, I hoped the children would change him. I now realize that family was never his priority. It was solely about perception: being seen as a 'family-oriented' person was important to him. He pulled the family out for special occasions to add a special touch when needed. Our job had been solely to make Kyle shine. After that moment, we were put back on the shelf until needed again in some capacity.

*****

"Do you know your husband likes men?" I couldn't believe I was being asked that question. I wasn't sure how much credence to give to the words. It was quite bold for someone to approach me with these outlandish allegations. I carefully responded, "Kyle absolutely does not like men. Bryan is a family friend and we've known him for a few years." I decided I would not participate in or entertain additional negative conversation regardless of how I felt about Kyle.

I later noticed that the disturbing signs many were whispering about became more prevalent. Kyle increasingly spent more time with Bryan. When they weren't physically together they were talking on the phone or texting each other. Kyle later helped Bryan to secure housing near the campus and awarded him a job promotion.

I began to feel uneasy about their friendship. Their growing relationship made me self-conscious. I couldn't determine what was worse, being cheated on by your spouse with a woman or a man? The thought of either made me sick to my stomach.

A few months later, we traveled to San Diego for an alumni conference hosted by the university. I was eager to make the trip to visit friends and family who lived in the area.

The university made the travel arrangements in connection with the San Diego trip. They booked a single hotel room for us. We hadn't discussed what the sleeping arrangements would be once we arrived. I was fine with us staying in the room together but Kyle wasn't interested in my presence there. He assumed I would stay with family, however I did not. When I returned to the hotel room the first evening of our trip, Kyle immediately left. He didn't take the key to the rental car we were using. He also didn't take any personal belongings.

I showered and prepared for bed assuming he had possibly gone downstairs to the casino. When I woke up the following morning, I noticed Kyle was not in the room. It was unlikely he would still be at the casino. He'd slept somewhere else.

When Kyle reappeared later that morning, I approached him for the first time about whether he was seeing a man in general and particularly whether he stayed with Bryan, who was also in San Diego attending the conference. Kyle laughed and questioned why it mattered to me.

I realized it was pointless to seek answers from him. He certainly wasn't going to share information about his personal lifestyle with me. I couldn't necessarily blame him. I wasn't asking because I truly cared about anything Kyle was involved in. I selfishly just wanted to make myself feel better. I was searching for self validation. The reality was nothing Kyle said could have done that for me.

Until you love who you are, you are incapable of loving someone else. It was a lesson we both had to learn. It became apparent that Kyle was guilty of living a secret life. There was a struggle inside of him as to whether he wanted to be romantically involved with a woman. Internally, he was miserable because he was not being true to himself.

On the other hand, I was guilty of checking out of the marriage long before this particular issue arose. The trust between us had been severely eroded and all respect for each other had been lost. Most importantly, I had failed to love myself.

One thing was clear: neither of us was happy yet we constantly pretended that we were. It was a sad situation for us both.

TIFFANY HILL

Chapter 6
BREAKING POINT

"You can put all of your effort in trying to make someone happy... But there comes a time when we become tired of trying to fill a bucket that is leaking from the inside."
~ Steve Maraboli

The alarm on my cell phone was buzzing furiously. I'd hit snooze at least three times already. I slowly opened my eyes hoping that the room would still be filled with darkness. It was not. The room was bright from the morning rays of sunshine. Oh great, I thought sarcastically. I knew being alive was a blessing, but I couldn't help thinking death would be an easier alternative. I was emotionally drained and still operating from a very deep, dark place. Another morning meant another day to deal with the mess that was my life.

I desperately needed to find myself. I longed for true happiness, not merely a carefully orchestrated portrayal of a happy lifestyle. I didn't know that by marrying Kyle I would be relinquishing part of who I was. I stayed with a man who loved his public image more than he could ever love me or our children. I sacrificed parts of my life, my career, my friendships and my relationships with family members only to be humiliated, lied on and to, intimidated and abused. I'd spent the past eight years constantly supporting him and doing what was necessary to ensure his continued advancement. I was consumed with anger that I foolishly made the decision to invest time and energy into our marriage at the expense of my own needs.

Dealing with the myriad of emotions depleted all of my energy. There were days I questioned whether I could continue to endure. It's easy to mask the pain, hurt, and abuse from others. It's nearly impossible to hide it from yourself. I would be forced to remove the mask.

Similarly, I knew that Kyle wouldn't continue to enjoy his fraudulent public image, his empty soul. Eventually, the spotlight will shine bright on him. It is, after all, his favorite place to be - in the spotlight - at anyone else's expense.

*****

Once Kyle and I were separated, the control and manipulation continued. I no longer lived on campus. I relocated an hour away from Kyle during the pending divorce case. Kyle hired a campus police officer to follow me around in the city in which I lived. He made video recordings of me and my children. He issued verbal threats stating that Kyle would ensure my demise. It was a grueling and stressful ordeal.

The university's governing board was made aware of the domestic abuse by Kyle and the fact that campus police officers were being used as Kyle's private security detail. Despite repeated complaints, no investigation occurred. The inaction by the governing board allowed the harassment to continue. It was as if there was an implicit stamp of approval of Kyle's actions, which served to silence my complaints and fueled the destructive behavior.

I was shocked when Kyle initiated a process intended to take our children from me. He began with allegations that I was an unfit mother and stated he was concerned for the children's safety when they were in my care. During the court process, Kyle testified that he had been the primary caregiver for the children for all of their lives.

I wondered what he was thinking. It was a very low blow. Surely he had to be consumed with guilt for the lies he told. Did he have a conscience? I knew Kyle loved our children but he was not their primary caregiver. His work schedule as president didn't even allow for him to have the flexibility he was claiming to have. In an effort to hurt me, he threatened me with what he knew I loved the most: the children.

Apparently Kyle was not concerned with how his actions affected the children. It was disheartening to watch him use them in his campaign to bolster his image. However, I should not have been surprised. The center of the story was all about Kyle as it had always been.

Kyle's secretary, Linda, testified that he blocked his schedule every day to pick up the children and that this was a practice he had adhered to for many years. A university daycare worker collaborated the fabrication with her testimony that I was rarely present at the daycare to pick up the children, neither was I actively involved in their lives. Kyle's oldest children stated that during his previous divorce, Kyle maintained a wonderful relationship with his ex-wife and was a devoted father. The lies were bold and apparent and having to endure the attacks to my character was painful.

It became increasingly difficult during the proceedings to listen to complete strangers with opinions about what they felt was in the best interest of the children... children they had never met; children they did not know; children they did not care about; children they did not carry in their womb.

I felt I wasn't at liberty to voice my opinion on the welfare of my own children. Throughout the divorce proceedings, my thoughts were met with opposition. My intelligence was viewed as a threat. Who was I to think that I knew what a legal standard was or to be bold enough to assert legal protections and rights? I was a young, African American woman who should be happy to have a working husband living a comfortable lifestyle. I was livid at the mindset they were displaying, especially when it coincided with everything Kyle had said through our entire marriage.

Meanwhile, Kyle was using politics to his advantage. He befriended a local judge to aid in his quest for custody of the children. It was apparent the goal was for me to no longer be a part of the children's lives. I could not understand it and at that point, I did not care if Kyle even had a life. I told my family, the day Kyle died would be a moment of pure bliss. I felt it was the only thing that could compensate for the abuse I'd endured and his attacks on me as a mother of our children. However, I didn't even think I could be that lucky.

*****

To maintain my sense of sanity, I focused on the children. I felt horrible for them. I tried hard not to let my frustrations show in their presence. They didn't deserve to experience what was happening around them.

Kyle began to make rash decisions in his effort to prove that he was somehow a better parent. My oldest son was forced to change schools to attend a location that was more convenient and accommodating to Kyle's schedule. The night before my son was to start his new school, I walked into his room to find him holding a picture his previous teacher had given to him. I put the picture in a frame and placed it on his dresser. We talked about the change of schools and I assured him that he would meet new friends. I thought I had put his mind at ease when I left his bedroom, but when I checked on him a few minutes later, he was holding his teacher's picture, crying. I tried hard to fight back the tears. I tried harder not to reveal my anger. I was extremely worried about him. 'What is on his mind? Is he anxious, nervous, afraid?' He was having a difficult time processing what was happening between us.

The children would go through many difficult changes from separation counseling to adjusting to various visitation schedules. I observed behavioral changes and feelings of sadness, guilt and resentment. I was constantly told that kids are resilient and they will be okay. None of that advice brought ease as I watched the affect our problems were having on my children.

Time and time again, I went through varied emotions- from actively seeking forgiveness and peace to furiously wanting to hurt the person responsible for my pain and the pain of my children.

*****

Anger! I had protective gear over my eyes and my ears were covered to muffle the sounds. I slowly lifted the gun and aimed at the target. The first shot startled me. I'd never shot a gun before. I stopped to catch my breath. At this point, I realized my eyes were closed. The instructor at the shooting range calmly asked me if I was okay. I took another deep breath, nodded my head yes and aimed again.

I'd spent the majority of the day in a firearms safety training class which culminated in practice shooting at the onsite indoor training facility. I was there to increase my comfort level with holding and shooting a gun. Initially I was very nervous, but my confidence increased as I continued to practice. To aid me, I imagined Kyle as the moving target.

I was so mad I could kill him! I replayed that thought over and over in my mind and continued to feed into the negative energy. There were days that turned to weeks where I told myself killing Kyle would make me feel better and I even began the process of justifying it to myself.

One night, I had a nightmare that awoke me in a frenzy. Up until this point, I'd repeatedly envisioned killing Kyle. In most versions of the dream, Kyle begged me for mercy and I still pulled the trigger. An overwhelming feeling of satisfaction followed. But on this particular night, there was a different reality. I pulled the trigger and Kyle fell into a pool of blood. I didn't notice the usual sense of satisfaction and relief that was normally present. Instead, I felt the pain of my children suffering. As I turned to face them, they were each looking at me in disbelief. They began screaming, "Why did you hurt him?" Before I could sort through what happened and provide an explanation, police were everywhere. Strangers grabbed my children and took them away from me. I had done all of this for my children. Now they were being taken from me. "Please don't take my children," I pleaded before I woke up.

*****

The bathroom. That's where I was. I wasn't aware of how long I had been there. My heart was racing even though I was sitting still. I had extreme chest pains and shortness of breath. My head was pounding and I was dizzy. I could not stand. I didn't have my cell phone. I was home alone. I needed to talk to someone and let them know what was going on. Where is my cell phone? Am I dying? Would it be better to die?

I felt horrible. It was a recurring sequence of being unable to catch my breath, feeling dizzy, experiencing chest pains, profusely sweating and being afraid of what was happening. I called one of my friends and explained the situation. Something isn't right. I don't feel right. What's going on here?

"You need to see a doctor," she said. I wasn't convinced that I needed to see a doctor. I felt fine most days and even that moment of panic lasted for only a few minutes. But it was still a scary feeling and I had no clue what triggered it. I reluctantly heeded her advice and scheduled an appointment. I learned I had experienced an anxiety attack.

My breaking point had come. Dealing with the emotions

proved to be just as hard as enduring what happened. I could not simply move on and think that things would miraculously fall into place. I had to dig deep and examine the decisions I'd made as well as the consequences of those choices.

I wondered why I remained in the marriage for so many years. It was time that I could never regain. I had to deal with guilt and own my part in the failure of this relationship. When things went from good to bad, I hadn't demanded that we correct it. I ignored abusive behavior. I didn't do either of us a favor in my decision to remain silent about domestic abuse.

I decided to be completely honest with myself and examine whether I ever loved Kyle. Did I even know what love was? Most importantly, did I love myself? I knew the answer was no. However, I needed to look myself in the mirror and face my truth. I neither loved myself nor was I ever in love with him. I didn't even know who Kyle really was. I rushed into marriage and ignored signs that could have saved me heartache later. I allowed things to happen to me that were disrespectful, yet I participated in covering up the problem. I didn't love Kyle. I loved our lifestyle. I loved the idea of the family image he created for us. I always hoped that Kyle would someday turn into the the actual person who acted the part in the role that he scripted so well for himself.

I wasn't sure where to start in the process of rebuilding or who I could trust. I needed some time to disconnect. I went into a deliberate retreat and only spoke on the telephone to select friends and family. This would be a tough road and I needed people around me who were genuine.

There were days where I couldn't do it alone, days when I didn't want to move forward. Fortunately, there remained a constant burning flame inside me that would never let me quit: my love for my children. I promised them I would never fail them. I would never give up on them. My love for them would be my strength.

*****

My cell phone was ringing. I didn't want to answer it but I knew I should. It was one of my closest friends. To not answer meant that he would be worried about me. So, I slowly gathered the strength to say hello.

I pretended to be okay, but the stress was apparent in my voice. Sensing that I was not feeling my best, he began to offer encouragement: "Get up. Fight! Your children love you. Your friends and family love you. I love you. God loves you. You have all the support you need. You can't give up. I need a favor from you…"

A favor? I'm going through one of the most horrific life

experiences ever and you need a favor? "Okay sure, tell me what you need," I responded, contrary to what I was actually thinking.

"I need you to walk to the door, open it and look outside. The sun is shining. The birds are chirping. You are able to experience it because you are alive and you are well. You are extremely blessed. Now, go look in the mirror. You are beautiful. You are a queen. You possess everything you need to get through this, and you will."

Chapter 7
FULL CIRCLE

"The most common way women give up their power is by thinking they don't have any."
~ Alice Walker

This year would mark the first Christmas holiday the children would celebrate without both of their parents. I needed to make the holidays extremely special in hopes that they wouldn't recognize that anything was different. It was a ridiculous thought for me to have because everything was indeed different.

I decided we would spend Christmas in Louisiana with my family. When we arrived, everyone was excited to see the children. The children were equally ecstatic about the opportunity to spend time with their grandparents. Their grandmother instantly went into overdrive making sure the holiday was memorable. They played games, baked holiday treats and enjoyed the time with their young cousins. Seeing my children running through my parents' home reminded me of my youth. The children were surrounded by love and they felt it, so they exuded love in return.

The icing on the cake was when they realized they each had their own Christmas tree for gifts. Three miniature trees almost proportionate to their height surrounded the large family Christmas tree. They thought this was the absolute best idea ever. It was beautiful to experience those moments.

We were in Spearsville, a small town in north Louisiana approximately ten minutes from the Louisiana-Arkansas border. We joked during our childhood that if you drove through the town too fast you might actually miss it! There are no red lights and very few stop signs. It's full of countryside roads with familiar twists and turns. I couldn't keep a signal on my cell phone which limited telephone communication and wireless internet was nonexistent. None of that mattered to the residents there. You became aware of the strong sense of community from the moment you arrived. It was a safe place; one where genuine concern for others was evident in every encounter. Residents would give their last to help someone in need. The entire community was family to me.

This trip home presented the opportunity to retreat from the craziness that was going on in my world and come back full circle to my childhood home... a return to my roots of sorts. It was very therapeutic.

Our joy was cut short the weekend following the Christmas holiday when illness struck our family. The next few days would be spent at a hospital with my uncle as he fought for his life. He was diagnosed with cancer and his condition was critical. The doctors had no plan for treatment other than to keep him as comfortable as possible.

We were blessed to see a new year. Yet, as I sat in the hospital room, I found it hard to focus on anything positive. I was reminded of how quickly things change. It seemed totally unfair. Everyone was together laughing just a few days ago at our traditional family game night. Now the smiles had vanished; in their place were signs of worry and concern. We avoided eye contact with one another in an effort to hold back tears. We were all praying for a miracle.

It was very hard to watch my uncle's health rapidly decline. Miraculously, he remained in good spirits, continuing to offer wisdom even through his pain. During his most difficult moments, he didn't give up. He quoted bible verses and engaged in fervent prayer. I was amazed at his strength and his faith. I listened intently as he told us to enjoy life and never take anything for granted. He shared with us the importance of leaving a legacy for our children. "Live prayerfully," he whispered, "for you never know which day will be your last."

Each day we gathered around his hospital bed to pray. To break the dismal mood, one evening we began to reminisce about my paternal grandfather. He was the ultimate patriarch of our family. We all admired and respected him. He was loving, but also brutally honest. As a result, we knew he said what he meant and meant what he said. He absolutely loved his family. He was the best and only grandfather that I'd ever known in my life.

When my grandfather died, our family was devastated. Not only did we miss him, but we also missed the family traditions that had become a part of our lives through him. An opportunity to reflect and share stories of my grandfather would instantly put a smile on our faces. My grandfather could neither read nor write, but often joked that he could definitely count his money. He raised a large family and was known to always have some sort of business venture going. He was an entrepreneur in every sense of the word, without any formal education or training. He possessed an unrivaled work ethic and passed that trait along to his children. As a result, they exemplified the core values that were now the foundation of our family. They showed respect and empathy for others. They were supportive. Their love was genuine. They were authentic.

It had been four years since my grandfather passed away. I could sense his calming presence among all of us. There was a message during those moments that resounded clearly to me. I absolutely could not give up. I could neither let my circumstances define me nor force me to hold on to bitterness. Focusing on the negative experiences would only rob me of my purpose and hinder me from discovering the true happiness I deserved.

My uncle's untimely death served as another opportunity to place things into perspective. I instantly missed his smile, his jokes and having his support. He never failed to express the utmost joy and excitement for every accomplishment I made throughout my life. He was there for each of my milestones. He'd also officiated my wedding ceremony. When he later learned I was experiencing marital discord, he prayed with me and for me. I found comfort in his words to me during the difficult season in his life: "God equips you with everything you need. You must remain faithful and true to his word. He never promised it would be easy but He will never leave you nor forsake you. God takes care of his children."

An inner examination of the core of who you are can be critical. It was time to shift gears. I was going through a storm. It was the hardest thing I'd ever had to endure to date. How I navigated the storm would determine my happiness. All of my experiences, whether just or unfair, were a part of who I was.

The return to my Louisiana roots was a necessary and timely experience. I owned the decision to be happy and operate in my unapologetic truth. Strength, perseverance and faith were a byproduct of my bloodline. My family was not composed of quitters. They stood firm in their beliefs and stayed true to who they were. That was the legacy I desired to pass on to my children.

TIFFANY HILL

Chapter 8
MOVING FORWARD, AUTHENTICALLY

"Authenticity is not something we have or don't have. It's a practice - a conscious choice of how we want to live. Authenticity is a collection of choices that we have to make every day. It's about the choice to show up and be real. The choice to be honest. The choice to let our true selves be seen."

~ Brene Brown

"You should download the Countdown app on your cell phone! Let's track how many days you have until this ugly divorce is final!" My friend was going through this ordeal with me. For months she'd been accepting telephone calls from me when I was angry, consoling me when I was sad and helping me to cope with the effects the separation was having on the children.

"Ok, I'll download the app," I replied. That's how the countdown began. When I first installed the app, the court date was over two hundred days away, which seemed like an eternity. Now, there were only fourteen days remaining until the divorce would be final. I was anxious to have this behind me.

*****

I was home alone when I received notice that custody of the children was awarded to Kyle. That was the determination of the court. The room went black. It was surreal. It was a major setback that I had not anticipated. It felt like another death; it was indeed a loss that no mother should have to endure. After days of weeping and being in a state of despair, the anger resurfaced. There was no legal basis for the decision. It was apparent that Kyle used lies to gain custody of the children and I would never get past that.

"If he has the power to make you angry, he controls you."

I didn't want to accept those words. Of course Kyle doesn't control me; I hate him! There was no way I would allow myself to believe that he controlled my emotions, but it was true. I needed to quickly change my course of action to avoid another vicious cycle of anger, frustration and sadness. I couldn't risk going down that path again.

I had reached another roadblock on my journey to happiness. The court's decision would serve as the ultimate test of my faith. The enemy uses what you love to try to destroy you. I could not give anyone that much power over my life.

Calmness finally came from knowing my truth and not wavering in it. I'd been an excellent mother. My children knew that and so did everyone who knew us. I had no reason to allow the politics of the court decision further erode at my self-esteem. I realized that Kyle desired for me to lose all personal dignity. I had to find the strength to walk in my own truth undeterred by his attempts to discredit me.

I shifted the focus from how bad of a person I felt Kyle was and concentrated on the type of person I desired to be. I would never succeed focusing my attention on people and things that were beyond my control. My energy was much better served by being dedicated to myself and my children. How would I find the courage to continue the custody battle through to the end?

I immediately replaced worry with faith and began to regroup to determine what the next steps would be. The legal process would continue to play itself out. More documents would be filed and appeals would take place. It would be a long process. However, I could not afford to wait until the process was over to find peace.

Paramount was the desire to be authentically happy. It became a daily mantra: You will be happy regardless of how people feel about you. You will be happy regardless of what anyone does to try to hurt you. You will be happy regardless of what the courts decide. It all starts with you.

Moving forward is difficult within itself. Moving forward authentically is even harder. How do you begin to pick up the pieces and not be ashamed of your story? What does it mean to live authentically? Everyone has a story but not everyone will feel compelled to share their story with the world. We should neither be held hostage by our story nor let anyone silence our voice. I'd allowed both to happen and I was determined to reverse it.

I set aside time for self-care, reflection and meditation just as I had done during my visit to Louisiana. For years, I operated in dysfunction and thought it was completely normal. It wasn't until I got out of the toxic situation that I realized how damaging it had been.

I processed the additional agony that was a source of my bitterness. I had discounted the impact of infidelity, homosexuality and other disrespectful acts. The constant lies and deceit all played a part in me doubting my worth and thinking I wasn't good enough. I had to let go of embarrassment and understand that Kyle's actions were not a reflection on me.

I had not attended to the emotional trauma I felt during my pregnancy and the condescending rants I endured; the sacrifices I made that went unnoticed throughout the marriage; and the admission that I felt betrayed beyond the divorce itself by friends and family members who took for granted the magnitude of their actions on the entire experience.

Every occurrence – whether good or bad – was relevant and deserved my attention. As the saying goes, "I had to face it to fix it." So, I sorted through all of the pieces of my life in an attempt to learn the lesson from each.

I started an intentional process of rebuilding my self-esteem and developed an attitude of gratitude. As a result of focusing on the positive things in my life, I began to realize that what I once thought were dire circumstances weren't that paramount at all. I had been oblivious to many blessings because I was focused on one subset of my life. Changing my mindset ultimately saved my life and helped me to move forward, authentically.

*****

There was anger lingering in my spirit that I failed to acknowledge. To cultivate meaningful relationships and, most importantly, to love myself, I had to forgive. Forgiveness of others was also necessary to engage in intentional, purposeful healing. It would be a difficult process and there were days where I wasn't sure I was up to the task. However, I had to seek forgiveness or risk being destroyed by the anger in my heart. I began by taking the first step, for I realized that the forgiveness journey was where I would elevate into the beauty of who I was designed to be.

Epilogue
SO YOU'VE BEEN ABUSED...

"You gain strength, courage and confidence by every experience in which you really stop to look fear in the face. You are able to say to yourself, 'I have lived through this horror. I can take the next thing that comes along.' You must do the thing you think you cannot do."

~ Eleanor Roosevelt

There is a reluctance to shed light on the issue of domestic violence against women by men in positions of power and influence. Those affected by this growing epidemic of domestic violence are desperately trying to comprehend how men are able to insulate themselves from any semblance of accountability. Women who date or marry men in positions of power who are physically, mentally and/or financially abusive often experience further humiliation during separation or divorce. More often than not, they end up voiceless, powerless and hopeless.

CEOs, doctors, lawyers, law enforcement officers and higher education administrators are just a few of the male-rich occupations that seem to be protected from any consequences for their abusive actions against their wives, fiancés, and girlfriends. These women find themselves as losing players in very public separations and divorces. They are often subjected to harassment and other forms of intimidation. Their voices are silenced with threats of retaliation, minimal spousal support is paid, and in some cases, custodial custody of their children is taken. Efforts to reach out to the proper authorities fail, and they are stonewalled and left to fend for themselves.

The lack of an investigation into substantiated abuse ends with an implicit stamp of approval from those who should be objective and fair, but who are more concerned with protecting the organization for which the abuser is employed or the image of the abuser. Because of his title, position and associations, the abuser is free to continue his destructive pattern of behavior without fear of requital from his employer, law enforcement or the justice system.

As an attorney with over a decade of experience, I am committed to the legal system being fair and just. It must be the voice for the woman who is voiceless against a man deemed to have privilege and power. Unfortunately, the law does not always provide remedies and protection. When a legal system ceases to hear both sides of the domestic abuse story and fails to make fair and objective decisions irrespective of a man's power, position and associations, it ceases to be a legal system. Instead, it becomes a fraternity of powerful individuals – and in most cases, men – that upholds the wrongdoings of one of its revered members.

I'm passionate about this topic because I have witnessed firsthand the victimization associated with domestic abuse and the struggles women face. When I refused to leave a harmful situation, I became guilty of accommodating abuse. I erroneously believed that I was stronger by staying in an abusive relationship: I was not a quitter; I was a 'strong black woman' dealing with a bad situation and persevering. Admitting that I had been physically harmed, verbally abused, and manipulated would require an admission that I had been less than transparent. It would mean facing my truth and examining why I failed to honor my worth.

As a result of my experiences, I truly understand that purpose can be manifested through pain. I realize how blessed I am to have gone through emotionally trying situations without losing my sanity. I am thankful for life, healing and growth. I am no longer ashamed of an untold story. Similarly, you should never be deterred by the fact that your truth might make someone else uncomfortable.

Do not endure incidents of domestic abuse in silence. These situations could easily turn fatal. Seek the counsel of experienced professionals. Contact appropriate law enforcement agencies. Ensure your safety and exit immediately.

Finally, do not let what you have gone through define you. Grow through your experiences and always remain true to your authentic self.

"The empowered woman is powerful beyond measure and beautiful beyond description." ~ Steve Maraboli

The National Domestic Violence Hotline
1-800-799-7233

TIFFANY HILL

ABOUT THE AUTHOR

TH Authentic, LLC
www.thauthentic.com

Tiffany is an employment law attorney and passionate advocate of female empowerment. She has collaborated with national organizations to develop formal mentorship programs and facilitate open dialogue on matters that directly impact women. She is also a member of numerous service organizations that have a rich history of cultivating female leaders, including Alpha Kappa Alpha Sorority, Incorporated and The Links, Incorporated.

Of all of her accomplishments, being a mom is her greatest blessing. Tiffany attributes her humble spirit to the tremendous outpouring of love and support from her family and friends who collectively provide a source of spiritual guidance and encouragement. She has a sense of purpose that is rare. Her story is an inspiring journey of triumph and the realization that nothing is more valuable than embracing your truth: "To live authentically is the ultimate form of happiness."

FOR MORE TITLES FROM EX3 BOOKS

VISIT OUR WEBSITE AT:
www.EX3Books.com

Feel free to share your reviews of
AUTHENTIC ME
via our website, email info@EX3Books.com,
or on Amazon.com.

Made in the USA
Lexington, KY
20 November 2015